TEACHING P

Science from wood

Dorothy Diamond

A Chelsea College Project sponsored by the Nuffield
Foundation and the Social Science Research Council

Published for Chelsea College, University of London,
by Macdonald Educational, London and Milwaukee

First published in Great Britain 1976 by
Macdonald Educational Ltd
Holywell House, Worship Street
London EC2A 2EN

Macdonald-Raintree Inc
205 W. Highland Avenue
Milwaukee, Wisconsin 53203

Reprinted 1979, 1981

ISBN 0 356 05073 4

Library of Congress Catalog Card Number
77-82981

Project team

Project organizer: John Bird

Team members: Dorothy Diamond
                  Keith Geary
                  Don Plimmer
                  Ed Catherall

Evaluators: Ted Johnston
                  Tom Robertson

Editor

Penny Butler
Macdonald Educational

with the assistance of
Nuffield Foundation Science Teaching Project
Publications Department

Filmset by Layton-Sun Ltd

Made and printed by
Morrison & Gibb Ltd, London and Edinburgh

General preface

The books published under the series title Teaching Primary Science are the work of the College Curriculum Science Studies project. This project is sponsored jointly by the Nuffield Foundation and the Social Science Research Council. It aims to provide support and guidance to students who are about to teach science in primary schools.

Although the College Curriculum Science Studies materials have been produced with the student teacher very much in mind, we suggest that they will also be of use to teachers and to lecturers or advisers—in fact to anyone with an interest in primary school science. Hence this series of books.

Three main questions are considered important:

What is science?

Why teach science?

How does one teach science?

A very broad view is taken of teacher training. Training does not, and should not, stop once an in-service or college course has been completed, but can and does take place on a self-help basis in the classroom. In each context, however, we consider that it works best through the combined effects of:

1 Science Science activities studied practically at the teacher's level before use in class.

2 Children Observation of children's scientific activities and their responses to particular methods of teaching and class organization.

3 Teachers Consideration of the methods used by colleagues in the classroom.

4 Resources A study of materials useful in the teaching of science.

5 Discussion and thought A critical consideration of the *what*, the *why* and the *how* of science teaching, on the basis of these experiences. This is particularly important because we feel that there is no one way of teaching any more than there is any one totally satisfactory solution to a scientific problem. It is a question of the individual teacher having to make the 'best' choice available to him in a particular situation.

To help with this choice there are, at frequent intervals, special points to consider; these are marked by a coloured tint. We hope that they will stimulate answers to such questions as 'How did this teacher approach a teaching problem? Did it work for him? Would it work for me? What have I done in a situation like that?' In this way the reader can look critically at his own experience and share it by discussion with colleagues.

All our books reflect this five-fold pattern of experiences, although there are differences of emphasis. For example, some lay more stress on particular science topics and others on teaching methods.

In addition, there is a lecturers' guide *Students, teachers and science* which deals specifically with different methods and approaches suitable for the college or in-service course in primary science but, like the other books in the series, it should be of use to students and teachers as well as to lecturers.

Contents

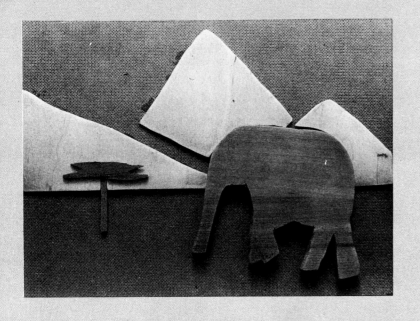

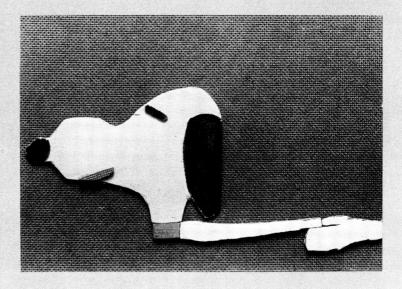

Cut-outs made by children aged ten

Introduction

Basic scientific experiences, like all fundamental educational experiences, depend on the contact between the individual and the material. The most valuable experiments are child-sized and wood is excellent material for such scientific experiences, since it has many properties which are appropriate for investigation and is available everywhere at little or no cost. Wood also has the great advantage of being a well-known part of everyday adult life. Much 'science' is artificial in the sense that it depends on apparatus and materials which children would never meet in their own normal daily life, and which appear to have no relevance to adult life either, for example test tubes and copper sulphate solution—fun, but irrelevant to most children and many adults.

The modern teacher introducing science in the primary classroom has some objectives that the pupils can and should achieve from it. These extend the activities and provide continuing gain; if fully used they help in the intellectual development of children.

Consider three Objectives from Science 5/13 Stage 1:

Ability to discriminate between different materials ('This *is* wood.').
Awareness of properties which materials can have ('What is wood really like?').
Appreciation that properties of materials influence their use. (You can nail wood to make fences or boxes; you can saw it into logs, and burn them; wood lasts a long time out of doors.)

Wood is a satisfactory material to start from. For one thing, the pupils in a class can contribute from their own backgrounds right from the beginning. Later they can invent and carry out many tests with a scientific content, some of which can also be quantitative, and in which variables can be isolated. The pupils develop their science from activities with this familiar material.

Some of the experience children gain from working with wood is emotional. Wood presents many small challenges to children and adults, and the wood sometimes wins. Children talk to the tools and to the wood. Woodwork may prove an outlet for aggression; a scientific attitude can be helped forward by the teacher, but it may be a long process.

Children can also have experience in problem solving. Here, indeed, they are often far in advance of a teacher's expectations. In their eagerness to get things done they try non-professional methods which may shock the trained woodworker, but active interest works wonders.

This book is intended to complement the two texts in the Science 5/13 series *Working with wood*, Stages 1 and 2 and background. It tends to apply more to the younger age groups, and suggests ways of using the most economical sources of material, giving plenty of hints for the non-specialist teacher.

1 Starting from children's own experience

The children described below, aged eight and nine, are in a school on the edge of a town.

Andrew, whose father is a greengrocer, knows exactly how to use a large screwdriver as a lever to raise the wooden top of a box, in order to pull up the nails or large staples out of the wooden sides. If it cracks the wood, Andrew knows how and where it happens.

Lynne, whose father is a keen gardener, has sawn branches off the apple trees in their garden. She knows a lot about bark, living wood and dead wood, and what the cross-section of a branch looks like. She uses a small wood saw, or a tenon saw which she says she prefers 'because the stiffened back holds it straight'.

Jean lives outside the town; the living room in her house has a fireplace with a wood fire. She sees logs and split wood every day, and has the job of keeping a small stock by the fireplace. She knows the difference in burning between damp and dry logs, how damp logs hiss, steam and smoke at the ends while they burn, and what materials (charcoal and ashes) are left when the fire goes out. Jean is the pupil who knows from experience how to make wood burn faster by giving it more air, also that the closed pages of a paperback do not burn because they do not have air.

Richard's family lives in a flat in an old house; they have recently found dry rot over the kitchen door. Richard is now an 'expert' and goes round testing skirting boards and window frames with the tip of his knife blade, to see if it goes in. Outside there are plenty of gateposts and fences for him to investigate. Next he may notice the rotting base of an otherwise sound post and work out why. The scientific follow-up, for which he will need adult encouragement, though not information, will be to inspect every available post. Is it always the damp bit half buried in the earth that rots? Does a bit of wood that catches drips from an overflow pipe or a gutter rot too? That is, is it the dampness that does it?

Richard will be able to build activities on his family's problems of dry rot, and do some practical thinking as he discovers for himself

The advantages of learning by discovery

Jerome Bruner suggests that learning by discovery has these important advantages:

Discovery means active involvement of the learner.

Discovery is self-rewarding.

Discovery learning is more usable and long-lasting than other kinds.

Discovery is learning how to learn (bringing an increase in intellectual potency).

See bibliography: 37.

What background experience of their own with wood can you discover from the pupils in any one class? Get them talking, and they and you will discover you know more than anyone would have guessed. This is something to use and build on.

How do schoolchildren experience wood?

Collect children's suggestions and get them to group (classify) them with you, using agreed criteria. Here are some possible lists:

1   As sticks, twigs, branches, logs, trees.

2   As fences, garden gates and gate posts, trellis, ladders.

3   As plank or wood block flooring, table-legs, chair legs, furniture generally, doors, window frames, shelves, firewood, splinters.

4   As broom handles, airer-rails, clothes pegs, sandal soles, play blocks, toys, lolly-sticks, matchsticks, some match-boxes.

5   As rulers, mathematics apparatus, desk-tops, tables, chairs (bent plywood?), cupboards, blocks, boxes, school musical instruments, gym. apparatus.

6   As orange boxes, packing cases, vegetable and fruit trays, beer crates, boards on building sites.

Consider these lists, and add other items which seem to you important. Then look consciously for wooden objects which have 'wooden' qualities, and sources of wood for children's practical work in the classroom. Organize the children to look, and see how conscious looking extends their observation and yours.

2 Natural wood materials

Hardwood and softwood

All woods are called either 'hardwood' or 'softwood'. Teachers should note this, since questions may be asked, though they will not need to teach it directly.

'Hardwood' means that the tree is a broad-leaved deciduous tree like oak or beech. The wood itself may be very soft; for instance, balsa wood comes from a hardwood tree.

The name 'softwood' means that the tree is a needle-leaved evergreen, but the wood itself may be hard, like yew. One can make the distinction clear in written material by using 'softwood' as a classification and 'soft wood' as a description; the difference can be made audible.

The activities that the teacher proposes for pupils depend very much on the materials that can be provided. Good material stimulates constructive ideas, so the teacher looks for all available resources.

Wood from tree-trunks, branches, twigs

'Natural' wood has always been familiar and interesting to country children, for example:

Tree stumps to sit on.

Logs to hide behind and to scramble over.

Branches to climb in or swing on.

Twigs to break off, wave, peel, whittle, hollow, bend as a bow with arrows, or simply watch for sticky buds.

Town children are increasingly deprived of such contacts with the real thing. In urban areas most of these activities are either non-existent or anti-social—even perhaps illegal.

Is it important to try to give town children some of the experiences that country children can take for granted? If so, which and how?

You might consider getting in touch with the local Parks Superintendent or Department, which often has to lop branches off trees, and sometimes fells them. Such branches and trees make wonderful teaching material.

Or you might organize a link with a farm.

The nature walk As an experienced teacher in Devon said: 'Bringing materials into the classroom is necessary, but taking the children out to the materials is better, if it is possible. Most of my class learnt something from our activities with wood in the classroom, but they all learnt something from our nature walk.'

How far do you find this agrees with your own experience? Have you ideas for specialized nature walks, such as a 'looking for wood walk'? This may easily be combined with looking for animals, such as squirrels.

What science from logs?

Firewood logs, unfortunately for the topic, are not allowed in smokeless zones. However, with luck, logs of some sort may be found. They give a good idea of bark, annual rings, heart wood, grain, radial cracks (as the wood dries) and splinter formation.

'Slices' say 5 cm thick across a log are informative —and make good bases for stands. Glasspapered smooth and sealed with a polyurethane sealer (varnish) they show annual rings which pupils can count and date.

A branch sawn at different points and angles makes a log jigsaw. The puzzle consists of putting the pieces together in the right order by clues of thickness and angle.

Large logs can be smoothed into playground seats. Here is information about age, structure and durability; also that wood conducts heat poorly away from where a person sits, compared with metal, making wood feel warmer to sit on.

Children's immediate interest in twigs

Flexibility and brittleness
Baskets, mats, tray-edges Some primary school children have made baskets, and will know what sort of 'wood' to use (cane or willow), whether it should be flexible or brittle, and how to keep it flexible during basket-weaving (damp). Other children can make logical guesses and try them out.

Coracles Can children get some ideas from a picture, and make a model of one, using a plastic bag instead of animal skin?

Bows These can be made for use with sucker-tipped arrows (with precautions).

Peeling There may be a problem when actually picking willow, sycamore, or ash twigs. because the bark may slip on the smooth wood centre, leaving large scars on the tree. (Pruning secateurs help.)

Peeled willow in the form of osier, withy wands, etc, as used for white baskets, may be known to children. Willow twigs may be available to peel and make baskets with.

'Totem poles' These can be made with rings, patterns, faces etc, cut out of the bark on the thicker twigs of ash, willow or sycamore. There is enormous scope for inventiveness and skill here, and some children will get very enthusiastic.

Totem poles

Art work As one Devonshire infants teacher said: I find using natural materials for art work the best way to embark on scientific method. I do most of my science by discussion while using the materials. For instance, "That twig is difficult to peel, isn't it, Barry? Was the last one as difficult?" "Why do you think the privet peels more easily than the elder? Yes, that's a good idea—the elder is dry, we picked it yesterday—but the privet is fresh. Go into the playground and get a fresh twig of elder; and we'll see if that is as easy to peel as the privet was."'

These were her comments: 'Praise some ideas without questioning them; introduce some "buts", but not too many or the children will become frustrated.'

She has a very important point here. It would be easy, as in mathematics, to let one's own knowledge and concepts run too far ahead of the children's ability. Do you find discussion the best way to keep in close touch with the children's comprehension? What other ways can you use?

3 Materials from sawn-up wood

Bought raw materials

1   Balsa wood in pieces, sheets, rods, etc, from a model shop.

2   Dowel rod; at least two thicknesses, from a wood shop.

3   'Half-round' and 'quarter-round' moulding.

4   Lengths of planed wood: say 5 x 2 cm, and 5 x 1·5 cm, also short lengths of board 10-15 cm wide.

5   Pieces of plywood: small offcuts and some strips (see *Working with wood,** pages 35 and 67, where pieces 45 x 2 cm and 8 x 3 cm are suggested).

6   Blocks of different kinds of woods, 10 x 5 x 5 cm, planed (see *Working with wood*, page 67). These may be used as reference for identification, but 'museum' collecting should be resisted. As Irene Finch says 'A mere collection of named woods can be a great bore.'

See bibliography: 38.

Free raw materials

Lolly-sticks   These have many advantages: they are free; easily sterilized by immersion in a small bucket of dilute bleach or antiseptic; of standard size and material (as far as wood can be); splinter-free; available in quantities. Collecting them could well be a socially positive activity.

They should be disinfected, rinsed and allowed to dry on a few thicknesses of newspaper. They are excellent as units for many experiments, from floating to burning, and their uniformity makes them specially suitable for quantitative work. They can also be used for making models.

Oddments
Scrap and offcuts from a woodwork shop or yard
Old-fashioned cotton reels (modern ones are plastic)
Old furniture, perhaps from the school caretaker

Greengrocers' trays and boxes   Some of the strips of wood from these are as soft as balsa, and cheaper. This very soft wood is not strong, but is easily cut, floats well, and though it produces plenty of splinters they are very seldom damaging. The trays and boxes demonstrate structure and strength before they are taken to pieces. Children observing how they are constructed may well use the ideas as well as the wood in their own activities. Thus the experience leads towards technology.

Taking the boxes and trays to pieces is a little risky, since the staples are often rather fierce. Teachers would be well advised either to do the job themselves or supervise it carefully.

Once in pieces the component strips and sheets of wood are best stored in a large cardboard box. Even the split pieces can be used to illustrate one of the fundamental characteristics of wood, that it splits

*This and all subsequent references in this book to *Working with wood* are to Science 5/13 *Working with wood*, Stages 1 and 2 (bibliography: 34).

along the grain (see tests on page 24).

What material will you get?

1   Narrow strips (about 3 cm wide) of soft wood.

2   Wider strips (about 5 cm) of thinner wood.

3   Sturdy little boards, often found at the ends of the boxes, about 8 cm wide and 5 mm thick, also of soft wood.

4   Long side pieces of thin (about 3 mm) plywood, about 10 cm wide.

5   Very thin veneer-type wood (rare), for instance as lids on lettuce trays.

6   Very useful triangular battens, usually at the corners. These battens are about 3 cm square, cut diagonally and often dyed red, blue or green. They are each something over 10 cm long and are solid wood with good grain and maybe knots.

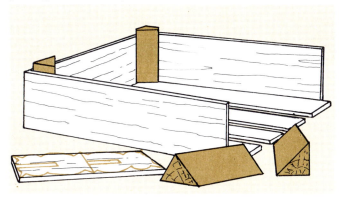

Working with children   Get their suggestions for sources of wood and for ways of getting help. Once they are personally involved there will be no stopping them. The next need will be for storage space and stacking arrangements: they will help with these too.

What good methods do your pupils have? Do you find that the non-academic ones have practical, if unorthodox, ideas?

Work with greengrocers' boxes

Observations of wood structure

Grain   Some of the wood will have split along the grain. Children will see, though the idea may need to be suggested to them, that all the strips have been cut with the grain lines lengthwise. Some will at once know why, but this can be a hypothesis for scientific testing (see page 25).

Annual rings   Harder layers are made when the tree grows slowly in autumn. Softer wider paler-coloured layers are between the harder ones; these are made when the tree grows fast in early summer. The triangular corner battens show these rings very well, because there is enough solid wood to see transverse sections at the ends as well as the longitudinal lines.

Note that the thinnest (veneer-type) slices of wood may show almost no rings or lines, as veneer is cut off round the log, like unrolling a Swiss roll. Children may well ask about this. (See bibliography: 3.)

Knots   show up very well. Pupils may be familiar with knotty pine, but they may not know that each knot comes from a twig or branch which has been 'buried' in the tree-trunk as the tree grows bigger. Some knots have their own internal annual rings, and a child may suddenly discover how old the twig was when it was 'buried'.

Plywood   This, the man-made 'strong' wood, is probably 3 x 1 mm thick in greengrocers' boxes. Its strength is a very important feature, and children can do simple research on it.

A small piece can be sawn or broken off, and left in water to soften the glue. In fruit trays the plywood is unlikely to be waterproof since the waterproof plastic-bonded plywood is expensive. (In some satsuma trays tested, the layers could be neatly separated with a blunt knife after about four hours' soaking.) Most children will already know, or will discover at this stage, the arrangement of the grain in the ply layers.

They can test its importance (see page 25).

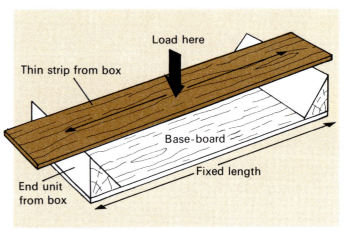

Experimenting The observations made on plywood lead directly to testing, and there are several attributes that can be tested. Starting with the simple very thin sheets, try the following investigations.

Strength This is the resistance to splitting. Is it greater lengthwise or across the grain? This is difficult to measure, but can easily be compared by trying to split the wood with the fingers. Obviously other things need to be as equal as possible. For instance, it would be fairest to take say two 5-cm squares from a single piece of thin veneer-type wood and try splitting them, one one way and another the other. Large scissors will cut pieces up to 2 mm thick, but the wood tends to split as one cuts it, that is before the actual experiment has begun. It is more satisfying if the teacher cuts up the samples with a Stanley knife on a thick pad of newspaper, though the point is made either way.

Lengthwise flexibility This can be tested by simple bending, or by bending to destruction. Some pupils greatly enjoy the latter, but there are a few obvious disadvantages. (*Working with wood*, pages 33–37, shows some practical methods of loading laths with buckets of sand.)

Testing on desks can start with a measured strip of wood resting near its ends on two of the triangular section battens from the corners of a grape tray. Loads (in kilograms?) can be piled in the centre until a certain measured mark is reached on a scale behind it, or until the wood strip touches the desk-top. Some of the longer thin strips will bend to the desk-top without difficulty. Would you think it necessary to turn the wood over and load on the other surface?

What variables could be tested this way?
Could you note the load each time and vary the thickness of the strip, or its width, or the length between supports? Could you compare the results you get with such wood compared with ply or other forms? What about dry wood compared with the same strips thoroughly soaked in water?

Any *flexibility* tests involve some quite advanced thinking, since as *With objectives in mind* says (page 44) 'experience of everyday objects often indicates that bendiness is associated with being long *and* thin, in a fishing rod for instance. At Stage 2 the separate effects of length and thickness are unlikely to be disassociated.' Can you suggest examples showing long/stiff and short/bending objects to help here?

Testing strength by breaking Here is an extract from a discussion between some eight- and nine-year-olds and the teacher about experiments on testing the strength of wood using strips from fruit trays.

Sandra, Vicky and Jonathan were very busy sorting strips of wood dismantled from some trays. After a few minutes it was obvious that they had agreed on a policy of making two piles.

Teacher: 'What is this pile for?'
Vicky: 'That's for testing; you know, breaking . . .'
Jonathan (guilelessly): 'Yes, that's where we put the cracked bits and the ones with holes in them.'
Teacher (perhaps thinking that here was another variable to be tested): 'And what's this other pile?'
Sandra: 'Oh, these are the good ones. We're keeping these to make things with—it would be a pity to break them.'

Consider whether perhaps this investigation on testing by breaking had not been made convincing or attractive enough. Or were the children too young for it? Had their previous experiences of not having enough of the good stuff to justify breaking it for an experiment been too strong for them?

How do you see this? Could you try it and find out if other pupils' reactions differ?

See *Working with wood*, pages 33-34.

Measurement

The kind of experiments described here need both 'scientific guesses', or hypotheses, to be tested, and also measurements in order to control the variable in the tests as far as possible (wood is never 100 per cent uniform). Lengths between the ridges of the supports and the widths of strips are easily measured; thickness may be more difficult. (See page 8.)

Methods

At least four methods of measurement could be tried by upper juniors:

1 A ruler marked in millimetres placed against the edge of the wooden strip.

2 A pair of calipers touching the two surfaces and then used to transfer the distance to a ruler.

3 A sliding caliper, for instance the excellent Osmiroid plastic variety.

4 A screw-gauge (also perhaps Osmiroid).

It would be good practice for a group of children to use all four methods separately on the same wood, then to compare results. Finally each should try out all the other methods.

Science depends on just such technological methods and on a reasoned evaluation of different methods based on practical experience. The resulting group discussion will be valuable and enlightening.

How far can you help children in the youngest age group you meet to see the point of testing?

There is probably a maturity factor operating here; do you find this or not?

4 Organization

Tools

Many teachers hesitate before taking on any work with wood because of the need for tools. Since a tool kit is expensive, it is best to collect only a small range, carefully chosen and of good quality.

A minimum tool list A   It is surprising how much one can do with a few items. Consider this list:

Fairly small screwdriver
Pair of pincers (small, for getting out staples and nails)
Junior hacksaw (with spare blades)
Glasspaper (sandpaper), medium and fine grades
Try-square (or set square)

(See *Working with wood*, pages 12, 13, 68, 69.)

The junior hacksaw is slow because the teeth are very fine, but this means that it makes smooth cut surfaces, and there will be few broken edges or splinters.

You will also need some glue, such as Cascamite or Evo-stik woodworkers' glue. Evo-stik 'Impact' glue sticks as it touches so the positioning must be exactly right first time.

With these tools and glue, greengrocers' boxes can be taken to pieces, and dominoes, pencil trays, stands, toy boats and many models can be made from the resulting wood.

Tool list B   Add or collect a few more tools to the first list, for example:

Small hammer

A few kinds of small nails, brads, panel pins
Bradawl or gimlet (not a sharp awl)
Surform shaver tool (as illustrated), which cuts as you pull, so hands will not get cut; it has one sharp-toothed edge (at the side) to beware of
G-cramps to hold wood firmly
Wood files, flat and rat-tail, for shaping and smoothing edges

Small cup-hooks and screw-eyes to match are very useful for attaching string, to boats for instance, and for making flexible links as in puppets' shoulders.

If the classroom has a woodwork bench, it will be fitted with at least one vice.

Tool list C

Tenon saw and perhaps a small wood saw (panel saw) for cutting up larger pieces of wood
Coping saw with spare blades for cutting out shapes (such as animals) from thin board
Hand drill and different sized bits (including a countersink bit), essential for making holes in wood (see *Working with wood*, page 40) as starters for any but the smallest screws
Small plane
Steel rule for cutting along, measuring and marking
Marking gauge
Pair of pliers
A simple Archimedean drill (useful and easy, but difficult to find)

Chisels   Some teachers in primary schools introduce chisels. One would need to be certain of the children's expertise before accepting this responsibility.

Wooden spring clothes-pegs   can be surprisingly helpful and demonstrate practical everyday physics. They hold things up on classroom clothes-lines; they hold sticky things together so that they stick; they make wires connect in little battery-powered circuits; they hold burning shavings, lolly-sticks and flat tin lids safely in experiments with wood-ash. (See bibliography: 7, 17.)

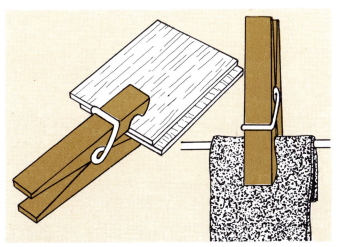

It would probably be very worthwhile finding out which children are used to tools, and to what tools, in advance. The problem is that they may tend to exaggerate their powers. However, some will have real experience, and this is an enormous help in the classroom. How can you find out?

Expenditure   If you have some money to spend on working with wood, buy:

Good tools   Cheap files, for example, become blunt very quickly.

Spares   Extra blades, glue, paint and varnish (keep sealed).

Pieces of wood   Dowel rods, batten, boards and 'quarter round'; also balsa, which is very popular.

A mitre board   very useful for sawing accurate angles (90° and 45°).

A resource pack   The E. J. Arnold Wood Resources Pack, for instance, contains many samples, stains, glue, polish, glasspaper, and samples of man-made alternatives to wood.

How far should one accustom children to having all the right things, and how far to making do? Perhaps it is important to know how to use the best, but to be flexible if you cannot afford it?

The safety of furniture and floors

Table-tops   Protect them whenever anyone is cutting, painting, glueing or glasspapering by using several layers of newspaper. Perhaps an old table-top, desk-lid or gym-form can be used as a cutting-board instead of the table-top. The loose grains of glasspaper glass may not be noticed among the dust and shavings, but can easily spoil a surface.

Using a bench-hook

The bench-hook This oddly-named piece of equipment is very helpful to woodworkers when they saw or plane. It protects table-tops and makes fingers much safer than they would otherwise be. It also gives confidence. See *Working with wood*, page 15; how would you avoid catching the table edge?

Bench-hooks should be obtained (made or bought) and introduced to a class before sawing any piece of wood smaller than a tree-trunk. The wood to be sawn is held against block A, while block B holds it steady against the near edge of the table-top. The saw blade goes past the right-hand end of block A and if it goes into the 'platform' it just makes a harmless groove in the bench-hook. Block B would be held in the vice (if you have one).

Floors Protection is vital. Against sawdust, water and sand (if you have to use it) thick layers of newspaper are cheap and effective. (See *Working with wood*, pages 24-25, 33-37.) The floor must be protected against falling weights in the same way.

The safety of the children

Probably the most important factor here, apart from common sense, is your own competence which you gain by using every tool and trying every manoeuvre yourself before teaching it.

Precautions *Working with wood* (pages 13, 15, 32-69) contains some good ideas. Also, consider these carefully:

1 Use G-cramps or a bench-hook for sawing: screw up the G-cramp with protective bits of scrap wood, hardboard or folded newspaper top and bottom.

2 Keep tools in known places which are easy to reach. Good solid trays or drawers with partitions are useful, especially in classrooms with little wall space.

3 Let only as many children do woodwork at one time as there is room for; crowded conditions bring their own problems.

4 Supply small hammers and watch their condition.

5 Make sure that every child handling tools knows about using them safely, for instance always keeping both hands behind or on top of any tool with a sharp edge.

6 Use a bradawl or a gimlet instead of the sharp awl shown in *Working with wood*, page 69.

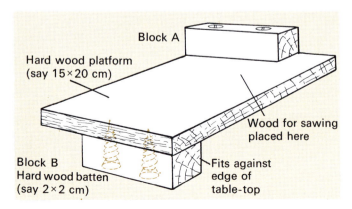
Block A
Hard wood platform (say 15×20 cm)
Wood for sawing placed here
Block B
Hard wood batten (say 2×2 cm)
Fits against edge of table-top

7 Do not use chisels unless you are in a secondary school.

Saws Good advice is not to push the saw too hard, but let it do the work. This will save many gashed fingers, as the saw pushed too hard, or crookedly, may jump. But with a bench-hook and a not too large saw it is very satisfying work.

A 'problem child' See *Working with wood*, page 18: 'Percy hammered his nail into the desk.' What you do about him is for you to decide.

What would be your basic precautions? Getting the feel of holding nails upright is important. A good early way to acquire this is to nail cotton reels to wood as wheels or pulleys.

See bibliography: 17.

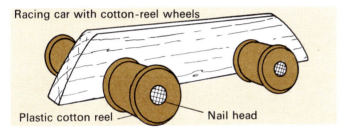

Racing car with cotton-reel wheels

Plastic cotton reel — Nail head

Problems Professional responsibility for pupils suggests that the teacher needs to think in advance in order to visualize problems, for instance:

The need for strength.
The possibility of sudden breaking or spring-back, as in extracting staples from fruit boxes.
The difficulties of small hands gripping adult-sized handles.

What problems of this sort have you found?

How far should teachers allow children to do things which may be a little dangerous? Is it the teacher's job to help them to deal with life's dangers by supervising such activities and showing them how to cope?

Children working with wood

What problems do you think children might have when using the available tools.?

Grouping How will you, or do you, arrange your woodworking pupils in your classroom? Make a plan in advance.

Does this help?

Helping children Look for and note down ways of helping children without doing it for them (a great temptation for the skilful adult). Does it help to produce either a well-made sample object made by someone else, or to make your own as a pattern?

Does a really well-made object tend to inhibit children from trying to make their own, knowing it will be less good?

A very experienced infants headmistress and lecturer said: 'I often have my children sawing wood—partly to give the boys a chance of moving around and getting some physical exercise.' At the same time, they and the girls learn a useful technique and absorb some physics.

What science? Look for the scientific and technological gains for children in working with tools.

Would you agree that with suitable precautions they can manage more than they are usually expected to do? Are you pleased or disappointed by what children can do with tools?

Behaviour A student who came into a class of ten- and eleven-year-olds busy with wood said: 'Isn't it quiet! There was much more noise in the history lesson I've just come from.'

There are, however, noise problems, and each teacher knows just what they are (the nearness of other classes, the head teacher's room, the music department).

14

Construction or destruction? This is a perennial problem, since a few pupils in every school are under great emotional stresses, and wood can provide a trial of strength challenge. Maybe the best thing is to take these children out and let them work them off? Students often remark that their own college woodworking sessions are therapeutic.

How do children react to tools? Here are some observations of children in an eight- and nine-year-old class coming to their second working with wood lesson (not 'woodwork' in the usual sense).

Anne, unexpectedly, had brought a screwdriver from home; she anticipated a rush for tools to take the greengrocers' trays to pieces.

Martin wanted to show everybody the considerable scratch on his left hand. 'I did that on Saturday, getting a box to bits.'

The children tended to fidget through the teacher's introduction; their attitude was 'Let's get at it— we'll find out how to use the tools as we go along.' How can the teacher use this keen interest safely?

Do you think children really take in warnings in advance? Would it perhaps help to work in very small steps, maybe just taking tools on to tables, then stopping for a word or two, then getting wood, and so on? Which way do you do it?

Science 5/13 Objectives

Stage 1
Skill in manipulating tools and materials.
Willing compliance with safety regulations in handling tools and equipment.

Stage 2
Appreciation for the reasons for safety regulations.
Skill in devising and constructing simple apparatus.
Enjoyment in developing methods for solving problems or testing ideas.

Further Objectives
Here are some rather more advanced Objectives, Stages 1 and 2.

Knowledge of differences in properties between and within common groups of materials.
Preference for putting ideas to test before accepting or rejecting them.
Ability to frame questions likely to be answered through investigations.
Ability to investigate variables and to discover effective ones.
Knowledge of the origins of common materials.
Appreciation of the need to control variables and use controls in investigations.

Look well through the book, and through work with wood you are doing with children, and see where any of these Objectives are being furthered. You can probably formulate other objectives of your own, which may not be in the Science 5/13 lists but which may crystallize out of your work with children and looking for science from wood.

See bibliography: 33.

5 Making things with wood

'Wood is attractive largely because children can make things with it.' (Irene Finch, *Nature Study and Science*)

See bibliography: 38.

The role of the teacher (or student)
Children will need your help since you will be their ally in solving practical problems: how to hold the wood still while sawing, how to fix pieces together, how to round off rough edges. The only requirement is that you know how, or are lively-minded enough to find out with the children. Some knowledge helps, and that is one of the reasons for this book.

Learning about children   A practical activity in which children are really involved is a first-rate setting in which to learn about children. You need to be competent enough yourself, by thorough preparation, to get the activity going. Then your good organization will allow you to see, as no education lectures could do, the characteristics and development of real children.

The children's interest   'They can get very involved when they use it [wood] to make things' (*Working with wood*, page 41). So let them make things, get them involved, and the scientific aspects of observing, testing, measuring, inventing will come easily with your help.

'Their interest stems more from the making than from the wood itself' (*Working with wood*, page 41). But the interest can be helped to branch out in many scientific directions: see 5/13 Objectives.

What can they make?   What is made by children with wood depends on a number of factors such as age, tools and materials available, fantasy, need, teacher, and so on.

Ask children what they would like to be able to make from wood, and think for yourself how feasible their ideas are. Try to invent ways in which they can be made possible. The children will probably be able to help you.

Construction from greengrocers' boxes

Consider what can be made from greengrocers odds and ends of wood. Also, think what you might need which would probably not be found among odds and ends—wheels, for example.

With so much free material it would be a shame not to make something. Let us start from the beginning.

A storage tray   Freed of outer paper and label-holding staples, a clean fruit tray makes a storage tray for apparatus and for pieces from other trays. The trays may also be able to be stacked. In this way children learn a useful technique.

A trellis   The bottom of a tray would supply a trellis for pea or bean plant to grow against, and to be measured against in the classroom. (Note: do not let the trellis shade the plants from necessary sunlight.)

A viewing screen   A single tray-end, with its two triangular section battens, stands up unaided.

Painted white or faced with white paper or card, it would be excellent as a viewing screen for small individual light experiments (using what Nuffield physics calls a ray box).

Scientific apparatus
Single strips of wood, chosen because they are reasonably sound, could be used for many pieces of scientific apparatus. For instance, the plywood tray side and some corner battens would make variable 'ramps' for friction tests and/or velocity demonstrations.

A beam balance
A firm strip, with a corner batten slightly flattened with glasspaper at the right-angle, would form a simple beam balance. The more balancing experiences primary pupils can get, the easier they are going to find physics later.

Scientific toys
Many toys with scientific possibilities can be made, from marionette puppets and mobiles to simple boats and catamarans. A single corner batten can become a cargo boat immediately.

What science?
Such a boat at once provides science by being loaded till the deck is awash, for example by inverting a second triangular batten on top of the first. The length of the batten (12 cm, 6 cm) can be related to its carrying power, for instance, in 10 gramme masses evenly distributed on board. These 'boats' tend to right themselves easily, and the tests can be done in small plastic lunch boxes half full of water so that each pupil can really find out what happens. Does soaked wood float lower in water than dry wood? (See *Working with wood*, pages 27-31.)

Tools
Taking full advantage of the possibilities demands a very small range of tools, and primarily a small saw, such as a junior hacksaw. Glasspaper (sandpaper) is also valuable, so that pupils may rub the edges on the paper to remove small roughnesses and possible splinters. (See tools, pages 10-11, and splinters, pages 20-21.)

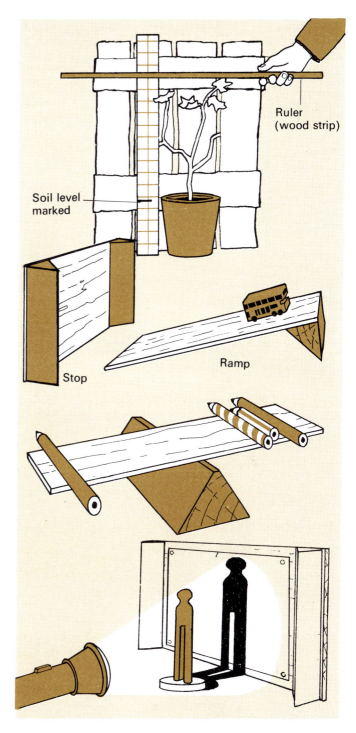

Ruler (wood strip)

Soil level marked

Stop

Ramp

A simple 'mass exercise' A group (or a class if there are enough tools) could produce a floor-sized class set of dominoes. Many mathematical uses can be found for them apart from the classical game. Planning is needed: how many pieces? The box ends, which are 5 mm thick, or the long bottom strips can be sawn across to provide 10-20 cm lengths as dominoes. Spots can be the adhesive paper kind from a stationery shop. A clear varnish sealer (eg Bournseal) makes a pleasant finish through which the grain will show as well as the domino spots.

Consider getting a group to organize the production of a set of dominoes from beginning to end, including the calculations and the manufacture.

Teachers often do too much of the thinking which children can do for themselves, but the children need to be interested enough to want to do it.

What 'technical' activities do you find work best in rousing children's keenness?

What can be done with bamboo cane? What science comes from it?

Here is a cheap, readily available material with many possibilities. J. B. Wood says in *Growing and Studying Trees*: 'to millions in the tropics bamboo is next to rice as the staff of life'. He lists some of its uses: for house and bridge building, furniture, water-pipes, weapons, baskets.

See bibliography: 6.

Model bridge building
Cane, combined with thin string, is excellent material for this.

What makes garden cane so good for structures?
Saw some garden bamboo chrysanthemum canes into short (say 5 cm) lengths with a junior hacksaw; use the pieces between the 'joints'. Then with a (blunt) table knife, try to cut the bamboo across—impossible—and lengthwise—it splits nicely. Note: put both hands on the knife, then fingers are less likely to get cut. (Thick folded newspaper underneath saves the table-top.)

Look carefully at the cut end and the split edges; the internal structure of the material relates clearly to its properties. Compare this structure with that of the fruit tray wood; cane is also a kind of wood. Looking at the sawn ends one can see the veins. Can bamboo cane make splinters? Try.

Learning about strengths of structures
For instance, look at wigwams: 'triangles are rigid' (see *Structures and forces*, Stages 1 and 2, page 19).

A roll-ball alley

Using this knowledge
Two wigwam-type supports and a cane crossbar will hold up displays, plants, mobiles (see *Structures and forces*, Stages 1 and 2, page 23), material hanging up to dry, screening for light experiments or shadow-plays.

Use rubber bands as 'lashing'. (See page 21.)

See bibliography: 28.

Look for ways to help children discover this kind of technology without doing it for them. They will invent. Make your own observations on their ideas.

How well does cane float?
Saw off some lengths, say of about 10 cm, and try. Choose your lengths to go conveniently into water-containers such as transparent sandwich boxes. (See page 28.)

A model Kon-Tiki raft
This is the next step. Use thin string or button thread to lash the lengths of cane together. The problem here is how to twist the string round and between the canes to keep the raft flat.

Loading the raft   Here is another good opportunity for *changing one variable at a time*, that is in this case the number of equal lengths of cane, to test if the carrying capacity of the raft varies directly with this number, all other things being equal.

How important is it to test more than one sample before you generalize?

Biological material is notoriously variable, and scientists are cautious. One of the small variables in cane, apart from its diameter, is the presence of solid nodes here and there along the length, where leaves originally grew out. These could either be avoided or counted.

Splinters

Splinters in fingers and knees are usual when working with wood. (The teacher should keep some small tweezers and mild disinfectant to treat them.)

Sooner or later someone will ask: 'Why did I get a splinter?' Does this question really mean:

What causes wood to have this property of splitting off into splinters?
Why do splinters happen (and hurt children)?
Why do I get a splinter when Brian doesn't?
What do I do that makes splinters stick into me?

Three of these may have a scientific answer. The answer to the third question may simply be that the child has an adventurous personality. The fourth question might suggest that the questioner is short-sighted or lacks coordination.

The teacher always has to look for the 'real' question behind the words, and to try to find a way to get it answered. (See also pages 35-36.)

Which do you think would probably be the basic meaning in this case?

Finding out how splinters happen
Investigate for yourself, and repeat the research with children, to find out why and how wood produces splinters.

1   Look at some ordinary split firewood; there is a lot to be learnt from it.

2   Inspect some old fence palings, looking for splinters and 'splinter-pattern'. Rubbing a sheet of kitchen foil on the wood with fingers gives an excellent result, but it may well show the lines left by the saw as well as the natural grain. The older the wood, the more the natural pattern shows up.

3   Get some scrap wood from vegetable or fruit boxes and make some splinters. This is one of the best ways to forewarn children because in this way they see how splinters happen. Luckily this kind of wood is generally very soft, and the splinters are seldom damaging.

4   Test your hypothesis further by consciously looking for splinters everywhere, recording results.

Do you find them with plywood? If so, where exactly?

Do lollysticks and matchsticks make splinters?

What about floorboards, wood block flooring,

table-tops, playground benches?

Preventing splinters
How can splinters best be prevented or guarded against, for instance, on small objects like wooden toys, and on larger ones such as furniture, doors and floors?

With children
Organize as practical a piece of environmental study as possible on this topic. Children will find it helpful at home as well.

Wigwam supports and a cane crossbar (see page 19)

What do they think of? Here are some suggestions:

Sandpapering rough edges with a manicure nail-file or strip of board.
Painting or varnishing ('sealing') to hold the loose splintery bits.
Planing, if you are using planes.
Binding (say a wooden toy) with Sellotape.

Give children every chance to think of solutions to practical problems posed by their own environment.

6 Classification

Teaching children to classify things 'needs much thought and flexibility; the adult's criteria are often quite different from those of children and may be incomprehensible to them. For example, so many teaching kits of materials for grouping into sets depend on colour that some pupils attempt to distinguish floating or sinking objects this way. Karen, aged seven, pushed to find an 'explanation', said: 'All the things that float have a bit of red on them.' Indeed it was true at that moment: there were an empty drinks can, a painted wooden block, plastic beads, a toy boat, a rubber ball. But the teacher was waiting for something quite different, and did not notice Karen's observation and the logic based on it.

See also *Science from water play* in this series.

Methods   How can the teacher help children to learn to group things, that is, to classify, without muddling them? Here are two possible methods:

1   Only offering man-made sets with simple obvious characteristics, such as Dienes' logic blocks (attribute blocks).

2   Asking each child to pick out one characteristic (criterion) of an object at a time for his/her own grouping, for instance that it floats or that it sinks. Isn't this enough?

What are your ideas on this general problem?

Discovery and physical knowledge   Constance Kamii in *Piaget in the Classroom* (page 209) says: 'The teaching of physical knowledge may . . . give a sense of security and confidence.' She suggests that when children are working with real materials like blocks sinking or floating, they stop looking at the teacher's face for approval, and rely more on their own ability to think. 'The teacher says "Let's find out," and lets the object give the answer.' Doesn't this seem like good scientific method?

See bibliography: 10, 41.

Recognition

Wood and 'not wood'   Zoltan Dienes makes the point in his work on logic blocks that the 'not class' is as important as its positive partner; though children seldom propose it, they understand it when the hint is given. The 'not class' is often a real rag-bag; for instance, in basic chemistry the non-metals category includes helium and silicon, while the metals group is much neater.

Try comparing wood with a few other well-known materials currently used instead of wood, and familiar to pupils; then classify them according to which are wood and which are not wood. It sounds easy, but there will be problems.

Recognizing wood   This is not too hard for children who have handled it thoroughly. They could compare it with metals, plastics (such as Formica), 'knotty pine' wallpaper (good because it shows that appearances are not enough). In every case they will be able to say 'This is wood,' or 'This is not wood.' A visit to a kitchen furniture showroom might be well worthwhile; then children can see how thin a mahogany finish may be.

One very good teacher said: 'My class all had to stop what they were doing when the "wood sculptors" discovered the smell and touch of sap. That was the most stunning discovery of the project!'

Science depends fundamentally on accurate, thoughtful, self-disciplined observation; the more experiences the better.

Comparison: wood and 'not wood'

Wood and pinboard are easy to obtain, and can be cut up into small pieces to supply individual pupils. This means that they can get the physical knowledge needed for confidence, and can then go on to use it for *comparison* and *classification* (Science 5/13 Objective: *Interest in comparing and classifying living or non-living things*).

A small group began like this: first they tried their own tests, then compared results.

Wood	Pinboard
Feels hard	Feels soft
Hard to push drawing-pins into	Easy to push drawing-pins into
Feels cold	Feels warm
Good for sawing	Crumbles when sawn
Has a grain	No grain
Can be split along the grain	If it splits, then it splits into layers
Can make splinters	No splinters

Try this with other materials, such as metals, corrugated cardboard, various plastics, corks, hardboard, chipboard, Formica. Make conscious, comparative observations, taking wood and one other material each time. Note that cork and chipboard are likely to cause discussion.

Why use wood?

What qualities does wood have which are appropriate to a particular use? Try out a few common examples for yourself and with pupils. For example, the wood used for fencing boards is firm, not too expensive, not too hard for nails, not too brittle; it is durable (in outdoor conditions), opaque, easily sawn to the correct length, grows in Britain.

Discuss with children (and colleagues) the special qualities of wood for specific purposes, especially by comparing it with other possible materials. For instance, you might take wood for flooring, compared with mud, stone, brick, tiles or concrete. Children have enough knowledge to handle this kind of consideration, and need little help if they know what format to work to. Here the teacher might suggest a specific use and ask the children to make a list of the reasons why wood is suitable, and also perhaps another list of the reasons why it is not perfect but is used all the same. (Perhaps the better alternative is scarce, or expensive, or indestructible and therefore 'polluting'?)

Suggestions
Cheese and chopping boards
TV set cases
Chairs at home and arms on beach chairs
Seats in the park or playground
Rulers (especially suitable) and pencils
Cricket bats
Handles on kettles and stainless steel teapots

The question 'why wood?' provides a good deal of science.

7 Fair tests on wood grain

Grain in wood is one of its most important structural characteristics; understanding it helps children towards Objectives from Science 5/13 *With objectives in mind* (Stage 2), such as:

Awareness of internal structure in living and non-living things.
Appreciation of how the form and structure of materials relate to their function and properties.
Awareness that many factors need to be considered when choosing a material for a particular use.

See bibliography: 33.

Tests

Seeing the grain This is easy when you think about it. You can see it in:

Cross-sections of logs; each dark ring shows the end of a year's growth (starting from the middle).

Floorboards, wood blocks, paling fences (see page 23).

The wood of greengrocers' fruit boxes.

Finding the grain Harder and softer lines are found by simple tests, for instance making rubbings on paper with pencil or crayon, or on household aluminium foil with fingertips.

Testing the grain The thinnest veneer-type strips from fruit boxes are very good materials for this sort of test. Here are some questions to ask.

Which way has the wood already split?

Which way can you easily bend it?

Which way can you split it easily into narrow pieces with your fingers?

Which way is it harder to break?

Finger and thumb tests, bending the thinnest fruit box wood, can be made more quantitative and therefore scientific by using squares cut with strong scissors (or a Stanley knife wielded by the teacher) so that there is no 'longways' apart from that due to the grain itself. See also page 8. Which way bends more easily?

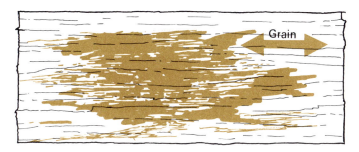

In which direction do drops of ink spread by themselves on or into the raw wood of the greengrocers' fruit box? (Obviously you can only do this test if there is ink in the classroom.)

Strength and grain

Now suggest looking at all simple wooden objects in sight, to investigate the relationship between the direction of strain (strength needed) and the direction of the grain. Try floorboards, chair legs, rulers, and so on.

A hypothesis is made here about the connection between strength and grain. Does it seem to be true in everyday life? Do children see the importance of looking for the answer?

Plywood

Plywood is made of thin sheets of wood like layers of veneer, but it is strong and often rigid. Collect information from pupils about objects made from plywood:

Tea-chests, which are strong enough to be used for house-moving, though the sides are very thin
Table-tennis bats(how many ply?)
The facing of some modern smooth doors
Many toys

Investigating plywood structure

The side panels of some fruit boxes (for instance containing Spanish satsumas) may well be of plywood. Soak some and separate the sheets. Check the direction of the grain in the wooden sandwich (see also page 7).

Testing the 'plywood pattern'

Can we assume that the arrangement produces the strength? Or could we test it? This is better scientific method.

We must isolate the factor we think provides the strength, that is the special arrangement of the grain of wood in the layers. Cut out a few equal squares of thin wood sheets, choosing unspoilt pieces (no cracks, knots or staple holes). Stick two squares together with the grain at right angles, making a sandwich. Copydex is a very good glue for this; place something flat and heavy on top for a few minutes afterwards to keep the surfaces together. When the sandwich is dry, try the finger and thumb bending test on it. It is probably stiff (but this could be due to the glue).

Making the test 'fair'

How can we make the test 'fair'? This is highly important in scientific work; there must be only one variable at a time, or the answer to the question is not valid.

Stick together two more of the same squares, with the same glue and the same pressure, but with the grain of both squares going the same way. Compare the stiffness of this sandwich with that of the first one.

What do you expect? What do you actually discover? Do you find that the children you teach see the point of making the test 'fair' in this way?

Some writers say that children are not generally ready for such thinking until they are about twelve or thirteen on the average. Do you think it may be a question of how it is put to them? Or does it depend on whether they feel that it matters or not?

8 Using wood with science in mind

This section is not intended to teach carpentry, but to look at work with wood in a scientific way.

Making science apparatus

Wood may well be the best baseboard material for many small pieces of science apparatus (see, for instance, the photographs in Nuffield Junior Science *Apparatus*). What makes wood suitable? Wood, with metal, demonstrates very clearly Science 5/13 Objectives concerned with using the right stuff for the job (see page 24).

Stands   Puppets need stands; model aeroplanes should not be permanently grounded; the weather station windsock needs a support. These are very simple to make, very satisfactory and quite scientific.

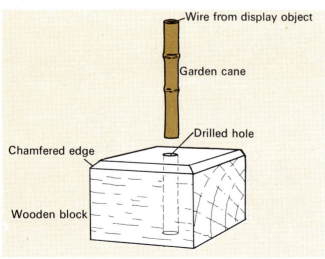

Wire from display object

Garden cane

Drilled hole

Chamfered edge

Wooden block

Take a good solid block (about 10 x 10 x 10 cm) of the densest wood available. The end of a joist may be easy to get from a building site, or two thicknesses of old desk-lid could be sawn to the same size and glued and cramped together. Drill a hole through the centre. A hand-drill will do it easily, with the block in a vice. Find a length of garden cane to fit, and drop it into the hole.

Objects can be temporarily fixed on the top by running a stiff wire from the underside of the object into the hollow cane. Chamfer the edges round the top to help it to look finished.

Children can do some of this, even if they cannot do it all. They could use a Surform tool or coarse glasspaper, or a small plane if they have one and have learnt what to do with it.

Science experiences   These will include:

Stability   The heavy part is at the bottom.

Leverage   The taller the cane, the easier it is to tip it over.

Nuffield Junior Science *Apparatus* contains many good ideas. See bibliography: 17.

Electric circuit unit blocks   These can well be used up to O-level physics, and the child who is familiar with them has a flying start.

It is not an accident that wood is chosen for this apparatus. It is not perfect, but can you suggest anything better? Think about the requirements, for example:

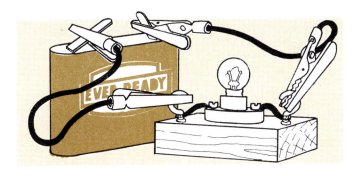

The material has to have screws put into it.
It has to be a non-conductor of electricity.
It has to be available in pieces of the right size
and shape.

See Nuffield Junior Science *Apparatus*, pages 19, 74;
Science from toys, pages 34-36, 68-69.

See bibliography: 17, 27.

Two-way science material

Making shavings for mobiles

Children can make certain wooden objects which will
provide two-way science, both through their
construction and in their use. For instance:

Xylophones   See *Working with wood*, page 16,
and *Science from toys*, page 13.

Balsa hydrometers and mobiles See page 32;
also *Change*, Stages 1 and 2, pages 22, 28-29.

Nail-blocks, dolls' houses   See *Science from
toys*, pages 13, 30-36.

Boats   These are probably the most productive of
scientific thought and activity. See *Working with
wood*, page 27; *Science from toys*, pages 40, 43-51.
(See also pages 27-30 of this book.)

The *Solarbo Book of Balsa Models* contains
outstanding two-way science models, for instance,
boats, bridges, balances, boomerangs, puppets,
a Kon-Tiki.

See bibliography: 22, 27, 36.

With colleagues or children make a piece of two-way
science material mainly of wood.

Work out ways to get maximum science from your
apparatus for yourself.

Try the same kind of material with children, and
compare what they get out of it with what you
yourself found.

Science from wooden model boats

Solving problems   One of the Science 5/13
Objectives for children learning science is *'Enjoyment
in developing methods for solving problems . . .'*. The
construction of floats and boats, the improvisation of
keels, the special points of catamarans, and so on, can
offer rich material for this Objective. (See also *Science
from water play* in this series.)

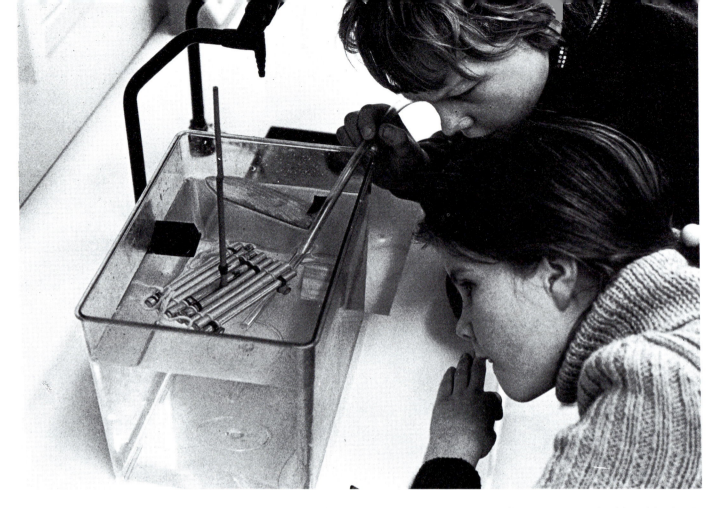

Adults can enjoy this with children. Pages 38-51 of *Science from toys* includes background information for teachers and many ideas and suggestions. Childrens' own experiments are described and illustrated, with details of boats with two hulls (catamarans) and outrigger models.

See bibliography: 10, 27.

Floating wood   Children making boats for fun see that wood floats, and that different materials float differently. They could be encouraged to investigate and test this as completely as their ability and interest allows. (See also pages 19-20.)

Comparison   Start by seeing how a solid block (offcut) of heavy-feeling wood, like oak or beech—

or even better, teak—floats compared with a block of expanded polystyrene cut to the same size and shape.

Woods tend to be too similar for the first experiments to catch everyone's attention, but if blocks of several woods of similar size and shape are around, tests may arise easily.

See *Working with wood*, page 27.

How do you show the floating capacity of different woods? By marking the water-line on the blocks? But with what marking material? And suppose some of the blocks float horizontally, and others float askew? Teachers should try first.

Lolly-sticks

Floats and boats: scientific method

Single wooden lolly-sticks, flat on the surface of water in a water tray, sandwich box or washing-up bowl, float well. They are very mobile, and make unsophisticated 'long boats' from which much physics can be learnt.

What is observed? That lolly-sticks float in water? How can this be tested? Push them under water, and see what happens when you let go. Do this several times.

Perhaps this does not look very scientific, but it contains the basis of scientific method: observe, make an intelligent guess (hypothesis), test it; observe the test results; correct the guess if necessary. The first hypothesis may be simply an inspired guess, a hunch on one observation; the creative element is, and should be, very important in science. However, it must be tested.

At the end the child says to himself not 'Teacher says wood floats,' but 'Wooden lolly-sticks float; I know because I tested them.'

Loads and instability
A small figure made out of twisted wire or Plasticine can ride the boat, demonstrating that the wood is really float material. It probably also shows up the instability of floating structures such as punts, skiffs and canoes, of this shape, without keels. Children will enjoy this too, and can be encouraged to relate their observations to real life. The word 'capsize' could be added to their vocabulary.

Lolly-stick structures: rafts and loads

An unstable raft
can be made from several lolly-sticks floated in two layers at right angles to one another. Friction may be enough to keep them together. However, as anything that sinks in a water-tray or bowl is easily rescued, this is not too important.

A Kon-Tiki type raft
can be constructed from lolly-sticks and cotton thread. Objects can be held up by it, though they will get wet.

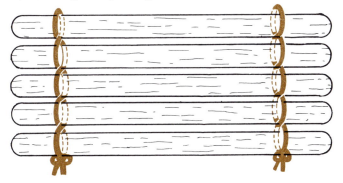

More elaborate rafts
can be built, with transverse layers tied together, with parallel bundles of sticks, with low lolly-stick walls to keep the cargo on board, or with 'floats' underneath the raft.

Testing loads
Scientific method can be used to match the number of wood units (lolly-sticks) to the maximum cargo load.

First identify the variables. One can have fewer or more lolly-sticks helping to hold up the cargo. One can have a heavier or lighter maximum load. Is there a connection?

Test this idea by isolating one variable at a time. You could do this by building exactly the same form of raft but using different (counted) numbers of similar lolly-sticks.

Then choose a standard unit of cargo load, such as plastic cubes from a maths set or Plasticine lumps of equal mass, with which the raft can be loaded to sinking point. Glass marbles are sometimes suggested, but are actually far too mobile. Load each raft in turn to find the maximum it will carry; do not forget to place the units centrally (more everyday experience).

Recording the results   Recording is another part of scientific method; it will enable you and the children to see the pattern of results. Patterns or relationships between numbers can often not be grasped 'in mid-air' but show up clearly on paper. Sketch plans or two-column sets of figures are appropriate at different ages. Even if the results do not produce neat exact relationships, the main point will be clear, which is that the more wood there is floating, the bigger the possible load.

Why less cargo?   As the activities go on, the lolly-sticks will hold up less and less cargo. Children will almost certainly notice this. Can they see that there must be a reason and guess (correctly) what the reason is?

If they have heard the Kon-Tiki and Ra stories they will know that the wood gets soaked with water. It is as simple as that, so you should not need to help them.

For more work with lolly-sticks, see page 31.

A bob-sleigh made of old school furniture

9 What further science?

Glue as a technological experience

Model boat building needs more than thread to hold lolly-sticks together, and Plasticine has real disadvantages. This is why glue is important.

Organization   Children enjoy glueing things if the glue is good enough, but of course the better the glue the more firmly it sticks to children and clothes (and the more expensive it is). Children are not economical with glue. Maybe this activity is for a few supervised children, that is, you join them. Think about ways round the problem, since they do need to know how to glue.

Finding a water-resisting glue   This is the first problem. Teacher and pupils together can invent very satisfactory tests for this property. A valuable one is to glue overlapping lolly-sticks in pairs with different glues. Leave them all for the same length of time; soak them all in water together, making the test 'fair'; and finally pull (or twist?) to find out which are more, or less, firmly held.

This could be made quantitative, but it is more likely to provide yes or no answers, or an ordered series running from the most firmly to the least firmly glued sticks.

Wood and glue   Many people seem to think that joints are glued together by fixing the wood end to end. The value of overlapping can be tested with pairs (or more) of lolly-sticks. Measured lengths (1 cm, 2 cm, 3 cm, etc) can be overlapped and glued. When they are dry they can all be tested equally to find the strength of the joint, perhaps by fixing both

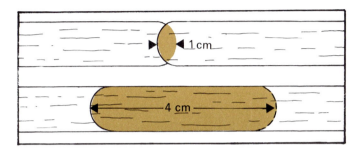

ends in G-cramps and loading the centre. See *Working with wood*, pages 24-26, 34-35, 43.

What factor will *not* automatically be the same in each test, apart from the overlapping length? Will it make a difference? Can you find out? Can you see any way of testing which makes the test 'fairer'? Do the children see one?

Burning wood

Burning lolly-sticks   For observation of burning wood it is difficult to beat scrubbed dried lolly-sticks. They can be held in the fingers until the last minute and then dropped, and they are easy to light. They burn in two clear stages: first, with a flame, to charcoal; second with a red glow, to the finest grey-white ash. There is good chemistry here.

Making charcoal   Any child can appreciate the black bit left when a match is blown out, and can 'draw' with it. The 'semi-professional' method of making charcoal suggested on page 50 of *Working with wood* is an activity for older juniors.

because of the cost of the wood samples. Pencil shavings from the sharpener are good 'fuel', but if they burn, they do so rather suddenly, so start with a small sample.

One of the best tools for children to use for making wood shavings is the Stanley Surform tool, which is light in weight and small enough to handle (see also page 10).

Shavings can be taken from different woods for comparison, especially of ease of burning; since the tool produces particles of the same size, this is 'fair'. See pages 10, 27, for making shavings. Mobiles can be made from shavings.

Left-over wood ash can be given to the classroom plants.

See *Working with wood*, pages 50-52.

Sawdust

Making sawdust is a satisfying experience in its own right; it is pleasing stuff, and its volume shows how much work has been done. What can be done with it? Here are some suggestions.

1 Burn a little.

2 Use some for school animal cages.

3 Grow seeds in it in the spring, since it is a good medium for germination experiments.

4 Use some for early filtration practice, instead of the traditional sand (which is bad for sink drains and classroom floor-polish).

Collages   Sawdust from different woods, light and dark, and different saws, producing powder or coarse sawdust, is wonderful for collages. Whole pictures can be built up with it, using only the weakest kinds of classroom glue. Shavings add to the pictorial excitement, for instance for birds' feathers, lions' manes, crests of waves, or sheep.

Organization   Allow for time for the children to get clean again. Always take safety precautions: work in small groups, and have damp sand and water buckets to hand. Slightly damp newspaper protects table-tops.

Making a wood fire from different kinds of wood
This involves many variables. Not all of these can be tested, for example age, dampness and the exact history of the wood, which might have been chemically treated. Results should not be taken as conclusive. See *Working with wood*, page 51.

Safety   Some teachers and parents may question this investigation as a dangerous precedent, so it is always worth making sure of your support. Take precautions as well, such as a small sheet of garage wall asbestos to protect the table-top. Note that its edge may be sharp.

Making wood ash   This can be done by heating shavings on a tin lid. It gives plenty of scope for observation, but is not so suitable for testing variables

A collage made from sawdust and shavings

Chipboard Sawdust may be requested or collected by pupils who have looked at the structure of pinboard or chipboard and who want to try making their own. A mixture of sawdust with glue (which kind or kinds?) could be pressed flat and left to dry. With luck it may resemble a 'man-made wood substitute'. The manufacturing processes, with plastic and a hot press, are not feasible, but the idea is the fundamental thing.

See *Working with wood*, pages 43, 65.

Weighing wood

The floating experiences (see pages 28, 29) may have suggested to pupils that they could and should weigh some wood to see if it is really 'heavy' or 'light'. Weighing wood is quantitative science. It is important that pupils should have the experiences of 'heavy stuff' and 'light stuff' long before they study density as a concept in secondary school.

A quantitative investigation Weigh pieces of different woods of equal sizes and shapes. The blocks of woods can be bought; a few kinds can easily be acquired from wood shops or timber yards. Choose three or four kinds, perhaps balsa (from a model shop), and three out of poplar, deal, beech, oak, teak (which may be difficult, but is desirable).

You will find that although the blocks are all the same size, they do not all weigh the same. It is not important to compare them mathematically, nor to calculate volumes and how much one cubic centimetre will weigh. Leave this till later. It will be enough to grasp firmly the fact that some kinds of wood are 'heavier' than others.

Finding the water loss of green wood

Weighing fresh green wood, as picked, and finding the water loss by weight illustrates part of the normal seasoning of wood before it is used.

Collect some twigs, such as sycamore, straight off the tree. Remove all the buds and leaves, with their stalks, and cut up the twigs into convenient short lengths;

the shorter the lengths, the quicker the drying process. Weigh them all together; you can adjust the lengths of twig to get a round number of grammes (say 100).

Put the twig bits on a tray near or on the hot water pipes or windowsill.

Weigh again when the twigs have obviously 'dried'. If the first value happened to be 100 grammes, the water loss figures would look professional. Why? The experiment should be repeated, since with such a variable material as twigs one measurement will not be sufficiently valid.

The first set of twigs should be weighed, dried, weighed, dried again (in case they had not dried out the first time) and weighed again.

Standardizing the results
Other twigs of the same tree could be used to standardize the results.

Comparison
Different kinds of twig, such as pine or willow, could be treated in the same way for comparison.

Children might think of comparing something juicier with the twigs, such as rhubarb. (They should not use giant hogweed because it is poisonous.)

All kinds of measurement are important in science, but children often get themselves tangled up in calculations outside a mathematics lesson. Is it more important to get a quantitative 'feel' across, such as about lighter or heavier stuff, or should the teacher work hard at the application of arithmetic?

Density
This should only be an experience in the primary school; the formal mathematical side is best left to the secondary stage. *Working with wood*, pages 27-28, suggests many good small practical activities starting from wood floating in water, and going on to scientific tests and comparisons.

The 'what happens when . . .' approach is shown to produce valuable experiences, and these are closely linked with children's real interests, from toy boats to Heyerdahl's Kon-Tiki expedition.

Water-absorbing properties of wood
The Kon-Tiki balsa-wood raft story suggests the idea of water absorbed by wood. *Working with wood*, pages 28-29, gives more outline case histories, and good suggestions for practical testing; variables are shown to be consciously isolated, and results are graphed by one group of children to clarify their findings for themselves and others. In fact most wood absorbs very little water, and children do not find much to measure.

Consider the stages in development of pupils you know. Where can you begin actively to introduce science in the form of testing ideas for the sake of testing ideas? Or is this a later development, following much experience of testing ideas just to make something work?

10 Questions—and answers?

Teachers asking questions

Teachers are always asking children questions. Why? Perhaps mainly to find out what children know, and which children know it. Obviously the other side of this is finding out what they don't know, and which ones don't know it.

Make up ten general knowledge questions about wood for eight-year-olds.

Do you think these could be really useful? If so, in what specific ways might they help (a) the children, (b) you? This needs thought.

Teachers may also ask questions:

To find out if children have understood what they have done.

To stimulate children to try some activity which will apply what they have learnt.

The teacher's planned question-asking should, and may, further help children:

To analyse what they have observed, discovered, etc.

To put together different discoveries and synthesize a wider, more basic, or more clearly comprehended idea.

To decide on, judge, evaluate their results and experiences.

There are two common kinds of question that teachers can ask. Take the topics trees, timber and wood. With or without the help of children, prepare:

1   A set of convergent questions which as far as possible have only one answer, based on previous knowledge.

2   A set of divergent questions. These are open-ended and in theory have as many answers as there are pupils—or more. For example, 'Why do you think . . .?' 'How could you try . . .?' 'How could we find out . . .?'

Both kinds of questions are necessary; the second kind is creative.

Children asking questions

Too little attention is usually given to the questions children ask or would like to ask teachers. This may be because teachers are too busy asking children. Of course, children often ask questions, of parents as well as teachers, to get adult attention or to collect support in an argument. However, the reasons for the questions may be far more important than the actual answers. Adults' answers are frequently unsatisfactory anyway. (Why?)

Collecting children's questions   Talk to as many parents as possible, and collect the questions they will tell you their children ask. Try to group these roughly into 'fact' and 'reason' questions. 'Why' questions are very frequent from pre-school age children (and also from adolescents). 'The word 'why' can have several different meanings. Here are some examples:

'Why did that branch break off?' or 'Why does wood float?' The question actually being asked here is 'What *causes* it?' The teacher may not have the answers for these.

'Why do people cut down trees?' Here 'Why . . .?' means 'Explain your (adult) motivation.'

'Why are there cocktail sticks?' 'Why do trees have twigs?' Here 'Why . . .?' means 'What is the *purpose*?'

'Why do some trees have flat leaves and some have needles?' Here 'Why . . .?' means 'What is the *pattern*?' This is an important type of question.

'Why can't we climb trees, pick twigs, etc, in the park?' Here 'Why . . .?' means 'What is the *moral justification*?' This form demonstrates the confusion between 'can' and 'may', between ability and permission: the children can, are *able*, to climb the trees, but they *may* not.

Studying children's questions
With children if possible, or with colleagues if not, collect 'why' questions, try to work out mutually satisfactory answers, and pick out those types which seem to you to be of most use in science, that is, those which could carry children further in a scientific thought process.

Nathan Isaacs classifies children's 'why' questions into two groups, information-seeking and explanation-seeking. The latter, he suggests, occur especially if a known pattern is suddenly not followed, and the aid of an adult is invoked to help in coping with the resultant 'at-a-loss state'.

The most valuable kind of help the adult can give is to find ways in which the child can discover the answer to a question from the concrete material by saying 'Let's see if we can find out by . . .' or 'Maybe if we do this . . .'.

For Piaget 'acts of intelligence' consist of 'adaptation to new situations'. There are two aspects involved: comprehension of the (new) situation, and invention of a solution based on this understanding.

See bibliography: 39, 41.

> How far do we have to think about each new situation as we present it to a child, to be reasonably certain that it is comprehended? And how far do we allow the child to invent a solution?

What does the teacher do?

Ed (aged seven): 'I've knocked lots of nails in to hold the sides on to my truck, but now the sides are all rough and I can't write the name on it.'

Ed was making a very practical little vehicle, but he naturally hit the nail-heads as hard as he could, and had not learnt to keep the hammer-head flat. What can the teacher most effectively do? Perhaps something like what follows here?

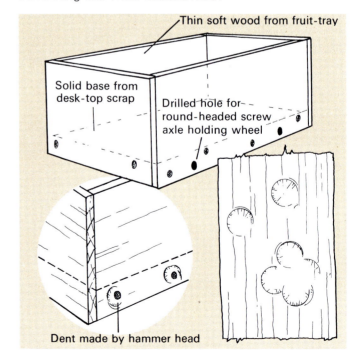

Thin soft wood from fruit-tray

Solid base from desk-top scrap

Drilled hole for round-headed screw axle holding wheel

Dent made by hammer head

Teacher: 'What do you think made it rough? Try just hammering another bit of the same wood that you used for the sides. Now look for those half-round marks . . . how did you make them?'

Ed was rather surprised to be invited to hammer, but went to work with a will and some noise, making semi-circular dents all over the thicker but very soft strips from fruit trays.

'It's the hammer does it,' he announced, avoiding possible blame.

Teacher: 'Well, can you make it make a pattern?'
Ed made a pattern by turning the wood round before he made the next dent.

The teacher put out a few more pieces of wood for him, intentionally including small offcuts of seven-ply and scraps from a very hard old desk-lid made of beech.

Ed: 'Miss, this one won't work.'

Teacher: 'Well, what's the difference?' At the same time she visibly dented a bit of the softest wood with her thumbnail. The teacher assumed by the form of her question that there would be a knowable, physical cause for Ed's observed result. This is one of the bases of science.

How would you keep the above investigation going?

For some good ideas, see *Working with wood*, pages 18-22 (the method on the right of page 20 is tricky).

Have you any other methods?

Language

Get some children working with wood, and listen to their questions and discussion. You may find that there is very little conversation since they tend not to talk much, nor to ask much, when they are really busy, and they may regard the teacher's questions as interruptions.

Consider how far you think children can learn in a scientific way without using words. Watch for testing of ideas, even when unexpressed in words; it often happens.

Are the problem-solving experiences they meet when dealing with concrete materials adequate, or do you think verbal expression is necessary?

11 Making wooden puppets

An easy puppet   You will need:

One garden cane
Junior hacksaw
Bench-hook
Table-tennis ball

Strong thread
Bodkin, or
Large wool needle, or
Hair-grip

First plan, then measure; for a small puppet saw the cane into lengths of 1-5 cm. You can round off the edges with an ordinary nail-file or manicure 'sandpaper' board.

The solid nodes in the cane should be avoided, though if a node must come at the end of a length, it can be bored with a gimlet (probably more trouble than it is worth).

Drop the thread through each length of cane with the bodkin, needle, or a hair-grip. Poke two holes carefully in the table-tennis ball, and fix the thread firmly at the top. 'Hair' can be stuck on top.

Solid wooden puppets   Their construction is well described in several books, especially D. Currell's *Puppetry in the Primary School*.

The proportions and joints of the body provide some scientific knowledge, but the most important principles are learned from building and using the combined levers of the 'aeroplane' control by which the marionette is made to perform complex movements.

See bibliography: 12.

'Flat' puppets   can be made with the wooden strips from fruit trays. Drilling or boring holes for jointing needs care, as the wood will split if it is forced. Good profile puppets can be produced.

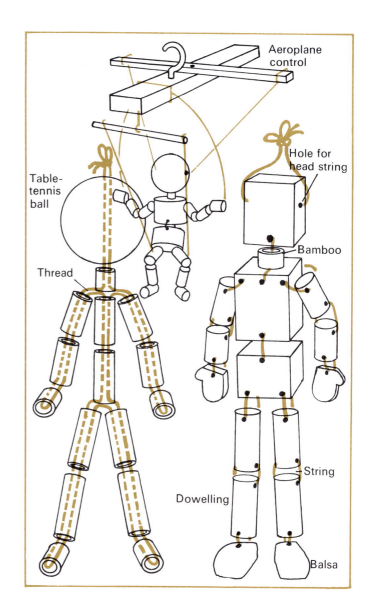

Aeroplane control

Table-tennis ball

Thread

Hole for head string

Bamboo

String

Dowelling

Balsa

TREES

Size Height Age
Rate of growth Felling
Branches Logging
Twigs Sawing
Sawdust Logs Bark
Homes for creatures
Shelter Kinds

EVERYDAY LIFE

Houses Planks Doors
Floors Joists Fences
Window frames Sheds
Rotting Preserving
Everyday things Tools
Furniture Boxes Trays
Handles Hutches Boats
Fires Gates Pegs
Lolly-sticks Matches

NOISE AND MUSICAL SOUND

Creaking floors
Banging doors
Hollow or solid wood
Xylophone Tapping sticks
Sound-boxes, violin or
guitar
Woodwind instruments

MANUFACTURE

Paper Cardboard
Chipboard Pinboard

Plywood Hardboard
Pegboard

WOOD

ART

Carvings Natural grain
Wood patterns

Wood-cuts Collages
Mobiles

TOYS

Jig-saws Puppets
Boats Trucks Blocks
Models Boards

SCIENCE

Grain Strength
Heavy, light
Floating Ashes
Hardness Burning
Bad conduction of heat
Apparatus Blocks
Supports Stands
Holders Rulers Rods

MATHEMATICS

Measuring Estimating
Cutting angles Volume
Mass Annual rings
Age and rate of growth

Bibliography

For children to use

1 Brooks, A. (1968) *Picture Book of Timber*. Hart-Davis Educational. Logs, wood, paper, etc. Good photographs. Bamboo, page 24.
2 Jay, B. (1960) *Timber*. Educational Supply Association. Timber, logging; wood in use; wood products—hardboard, shavings, etc.
3 Larkman, B. (1973) *Woodwork*. Ladybird 'How to do it' series. Wills & Hepworth. Lots of tools, pictures and information. See especially pages 16, 17.
4 Macdonald Junior Reference Library (1970) *Timber*. Macdonald Educational. Timber A-Z; uses of wood; plywood, blockwood. Knots, page 29.
5 Williams, C. (1972) *Trees*. Picture Information Books. A. & C. Black. Wood and its uses; man and forest.
6 Wood, J. B. (1966) *Growing and Studying Trees*. Rural Studies Series. Book 8, Blandford. Redwood trunk with 1045 annual rings and dates; tables of timbers and uses; bamboo, page 29.
7 Wynter, E. J. (1974) *Using Woodwork Tools*. A. & C. Black. See page 46.

For direct work with children

8 Bainbridge, J. W., Stockdale, R. W., and Wastnedge, E. R. (1970) *Junior Science Source Book*. Collins. See pages 96-98, 198-200.
9 Bayley, T. (1966) *The Craft of Model Making*. Dryad. Especially good on animals.
10 Bird, J. (1976) *Science from water play*. Nuffield/Chelsea College Teaching Primary Science series. Macdonald Educational.
11 Catford, N. (1969) *Making Nursery Toys*. Elek.
12 Currell, D. (1970) *Puppetry in the Primary School*. Batsford.
13 Diamond, D. (1975) *Seeds and seedlings*. Nuffield/Chelsea College Teaching Primary Science series. Macdonald Educational.
14 Horton, W. M. (1966) *Wooden Toy-making*. 7th edition. Dryad. Fun.
15 Mathias, B. (1974) *Simple Wooden Toy-making*. Hamlyn. Animals, trucks, dolls' houses, etc.
16 Nuffield Junior Science (1967) *Animals and Plants*. Collins. See pages 35-46, 90-95, 114, 192-193, 214, 277-280.
17 Nuffield Junior Science (1967) *Apparatus*. Collins. Uses of wood throughout. See especially pages 37, 164.
18 Nuffield Junior Science (1967) *Teachers' Guide 1*. Collins. See pages 30-31, 37-38, 61, 84, 93-94, 115-117, 124, 156, 191, 241, 277-278.
19 Nuffield Junior Science (1967) *Teachers' Guide 2*. Collins. See page 77.
20 Nuffield Secondary Science (1971) *Theme 7 Using Materials*. (Secondary school.) See pages 138, 140-141, 143, 146, 159.
21 Petersen, G. (1967) *Making Toys with Plywood*. Reinhold. Good, but not easy.
22 Schools Council Science 5/13 (1973) *Change*, Stages 1 and 2 and background. Macdonald Educational.
23 Schools Council Science 5/13 (1972) *Early experiences*. Macdonald Educational. See pages 21-23, 35, 69.
24 Schools Council Science 5/13 (1973) *Holes, gaps and cavities*, Stages 1 and 2. Macdonald Educational.
25 Schools Council Science 5/13 (1973) *Metals*, Stages 1 and 2. Macdonald Educational.
26 Schools Council Science 5/13 (1973) *Minibeasts*, stages 1 and 2. Macdonald Educational.

27 Schools Council Science 5/13 (1972) *Science from Toys*, Stages 1 and 2. Macdonald Educational.
28 Schools Council Science 5/13 (1973) *Structures and forces*, Stages 1 and 2. Macdonald Educational.
29 Schools Council Science 5/13 (1972) *Time*, Stages 1 and 2 and background. Macdonald Educational.
30 Schools Council Science 5/13 (1973) *Trees*, Stages 1 and 2. See pages 52, 65. Macdonald Educational.
31 Schools Council Science 5/13 (1974) *Using the environment 2 Investigations*, Part 1. Macdonald Educational. See Chapters 4 and 6.
32 Schools Council Science 5/13 (1974) *Using the environment 3 Tackling problems*, Part 1. Macdonald Educational. See pages 36, 38.
33 Schools Council Science 5/13 (1972) *With objectives in mind*. Macdonald Educational. See pages 23-25.
34 Schools Council Science 5/13 (1972) *Working with wood*, Stages 1 and 2.
35 Snook, B. (1965) *Puppets*. Batsford. Attractive and practical.
36 *Solarbo Book of Balsa Models* (1969). Model and Allied Publications.

For uses of wood as baseboard or support for apparatus, see nos 24, 25, 26, 27, 28, 29.

For further information and ideas

37 Carin, A. A. and Sund, R. B. (1970) *Teaching Science through Discovery*. 2nd edition. Merrill.
38 Finch, I. (1971) *Nature Study and Science*. Longman.
39 Isaacs, N. (1969) *Early Scientific Trends in Children*. 5th edition. National Froebel Foundation.
40 Kuslan, L. I. and Stone, A. H. (1973) *Teaching Children Science: An Inquiry Approach*. 2nd edition. Wadsworth.
41 Schwebel, M. and Raph, J. (eds.) (1973) *Piaget in the Classroom*. Routledge & Kegan Paul. Pages 216, 276.
42 Thier, H. D. (1971) *Teaching Elementary School Science: A Laboratory Approach*. D. C. Heath.

Acknowledgements

The author and publishers gratefully acknowledge the help given by:

The staff and pupils of:

Little Ealing Middle School, London W5

Students of Thomas Huxley College, London W3

Illustration credits

Photographs by Terry Williams

Line drawings by GWA Design Consultants

Cover design by GWA Design Consultants

Index